Copyright © 1998 by Universal Studios Publishing Rights, a division of Universal
Studios Licensing, Inc. Babe, Babe: Pig in the City, Babe and Friends, and all related
characters are copyrights and trademarks of Universal City Studios, Inc.
www. universalstudios. com
All rights reserved.
Published in the United States by Random House, Inc. , New York, and
simultaneously in Canada by Random House of Canada Limited, Toronto.
www. randomhouse. com/ kids
ISBN: 0-679-89447-0
Library of Congress Catalog Card Number: 98-67198
Printed in the United States of America 10 9 8 7 6 5 4 3 2 1

THE WRLD ACCORDING TO BABE AND FRIENDS

Quotations selected from the
motion picture screenplays

BABE: A Little Pig Goes a Long Way

written by George Miller & Chris Noonan
based on the book by Dick King-Smith

and

BABE: Pig in the City

written by
George Miller   Judy Morris   Mark Lamprell
based on characters created by Dick King-Smith

THE W RLD ACCORDING TO *BABE* AND FRIENDS

DOWN ON THE FARM

On Pigs

Pigs is pigs and dogs is dogs.

COW

Not as stupid as sheep, mind you,
but they're definitely stupid.

FLY

An inconsequential species with no
other purpose than to be eaten by humans.

THELONIUS

Pigs don't have a purpose.

DUCHESS

A pig's proper place is in the mud wallow
by the pond. Not in the garden.
And absolutely never in the house.

REX

Pigs aren't
built to fly.

FLY

Pigs actually prefer a leftover.

BABE

You're a pig. Your job's to
stay here and eat your food.

FLY

Pigs have rights.

FERDINAND

...On Dogs

The dogs are here
to help the Boss's husband
with the sheep.

DUCHESS

Treat you like dirt,
they do.
Bite you as soon as
look at you,
the savages.

MAA

It's a dog-eat-dog world,
and there's not enough dog
to go around.

ZOOTIE

No brains, no heart.

MAA

...On Cats

I'm here to be beautiful and
affectionate to the Boss.

DUCHESS

Humans don't eat cats.
Why?
They're indispensable—
they catch mice.

FERDINAND

I'm allergic to cats.

FERDINAND

There are many perfectly nice cats in
the world. But there are bad apples in any
barrel, and it is well to heed the old adage:
Beware the bad cat bearing a grudge.

NARRATOR

Don't worry.
I won't wake the cat.

BABE

...and Ducks

Being a duck,
he must behave like a duck.
No more of this crowing nonsense.

REX

Never listen to the delirious drivel of
a demented duck.

COW

Humans eat ducks.

FERDINAND

Ducks don't have a purpose.

DUCHESS

...and Roosters

Humans don't eat roosters.
Why?
They wake everyone up
in the morning.

FERDINAND

Of Sheep and Men

Time's too precious to
waste it on a sheep.

FLY

Sheeps is animals with thick woolly coats.

SKIP

And thick woolly heads!

TRIP

And men can't look after them
without us.

The Bosses only eat
stupid animals like sheep and
ducks and chickens.

If I could say what went on
in the minds of men,
wouldn't I be a wise old sheep!

EVERY-BODY HAS AN OPINION

On Facts and Nature

We can't meddle with the natural order.

REX

It was a cold fact of nature that sheep
were stupid, and no one would ever
persuade her otherwise.

NARRATOR (ABOUT FLY)

It was a cold fact of nature that wolves
were ignorant, and nothing would
convince them otherwise.

NARRATOR (ABOUT SHEEP)

Believe me, sooner or later
every pig gets eaten.
That's the way the world works.

DUCHESS

.

The fact is that animals that don't seem to
have a purpose really do have a purpose.
The Bosses have to eat. It's probably the most
noble purpose of all when you come to
think about it.

DUCHESS

The Way Things Are

That's just the way
things are.

FLY

The way
things are
stinks.

FERDINAND

The only place
you'll find happiness is
within yourself.

And the only way
you'll find it there is
to accept that the
way things are is
the way things are.

COW

On Babe

You look like an intelligent, sophisticated,
discerning young fellow.

FERDINAND

He's just a
little pig.

FLY

A heart o' gold.

MAA

What lovely ma-a-a-a-anners!

BLACK SHEEP

One little pig isn't going to
change the world.

DUCHESS

He's my good-luck pig.

FERDINAND

You must have a very thin grasp on reality.
Unless, of course, you're suicidal.

DOBERMAN

I know you're different from the others.

PINK POODLE

It's. . . er. . .
kind of a baldy, pinky,
whitey thingy.

ZOOTIE

But he's practically human.

MRS. HOGGETT

The Reality of Babe
(according to Babe)

I'm not a wolf.

I'm not a sheepdog.

I'm not a puppy. I'm a sheep-pig.

I am not a Cutey Pie, either.
I am not any kind of pie.
I'm a pig on a mission.

I may be small, but I can be
ferocious if provoked.

Do I look like a cat?

On Alarm Clocks

What a splendid way to
wake up each morning!

MRS. HOGGETT

The treachery of it!
A mechanical rooster!

FERDINAND

AMUSING
MUSINGS

On Farms

There's a place I know
where everyone is inclined
to be good and fair.

BABE

Nowhere to go,
nowhere to hide.
Here, at least,
a feller's got a
sporting chance.

FERDINAND

On Time

The time comes for all creatures
when childhood ends and the doorway
opens to life as an adult.

NARRATOR

Being young, it's hard to discriminate.

REX

The past is gone.

BOB

On Humans

They make the world work.

THELONIUS

Some people are so touchy.

MRS. HOGGETT

On Haircuts

The difference between a
good haircut and a bad haircut
is just a couple of weeks.

REX

On Technology

I think it's a lovely fax machine,
darling,
but can't you use it?

MRS. HOGGETT

You need to modernize,
get some sort of cash flow going.

THE HOGGETTS' SON-IN-LAW

On Sickness

Sickness can make you see things
in strange ways.

NARRATOR

It's not distemper,
it can't be rabies, so it must be
the hormones.

THE VET

I'm told there are
very good tablets for this sort
of thing nowadays.

FRIEND OF MRS. HOGGETT'S

On Healing

A kind and steady heart can
mend a sorry world.

NARRATOR

You can't undo what's
happened, son, but you can
make up for it.

REX

Sometimes two broken halves can
make something afresh . . .
something more complete.

NARRATOR

On Talent and Skill

Sometimes we discover our talents
only through necessity.

NARRATOR

What some folks lack in skill
they make up for in determination.

NARRATOR

You could be a sniffer
with a schnoz like that.

BEAGLE

On Heroism

The first hazard for
the returning hero is fame.

NARRATOR

More often than not in this
uncertain world,
fortune favors the brave.

FLY

ADVICE
IS NICE

Sage Advice

If you can't say anything nice,
don't say anything at all!

BABE

Do not take counsel of your fears.

REX

Cats and dogs
should be nicer to
each other.

BABE

Don't be afraid of it just because it's new.

THE HOGGETTS' DAUGHTER

Listen to your big brother.

ZOOTIE

Don't judge . . . too harshly.

FLY

Stay calm, maintain a tight formation,
and proceed in an orderly fashion.

BABE

Learn restraint.

THELONIUS

Don't do anything you don't want to.

FERDINAND

How to Succeed as a Sheepdog
(according to Fly)

But speed isn't the thing. It's attitude.
They just have to know who's boss.

Remember. You have to *dominate* them.

We're their masters, Babe.
Let them doubt it for a second
and they'll walk all over you.

Be ruthless! Whatever it takes!
Bend them to your will!

How to Succeed as a Sheepdog
(according to Maa)

All a nice little chap
like you need do
is ask.

Ferdinand's List of Things to Remember

Fat ... is ... fatal!

Christmas ... means ... carnage!

Most ducks prefer to forget it,
but the fact is that humans like to
eat plump, attractive ducks.

Don't cross
your bridges until
they hatch.

Ferdinand's Tips and Quips on Self-Preservation

I'm not going to be a goner, so I'm gone.

I s'pose the life of an anorexic duck doesn't amount to much in the broad scheme of things, but, Babe, I'm all I've got.

My life is in your hands.
(to Babe)

I'm a clever duck.
I could do with an adventure.

ALL ABOUT
RULES

Rules to Remember

No felines on this floor.

You must be here by 3:30,
or you'll be disqualified.

Only dogs and cats inside the house.

FLY

No animals in the airport.

AIRPORT SECURITY GUARD

Never answer the front door.

LANDLADY

...and What Is Thought of Them

It's against the rules.

BABE

I like that rule. It's a good rule.
But this is bigger than rules.
This is life and death!

FERDINAND

The committee has ruled that
if you wish to proceed, there is nothing
that we can do to stop you.

CHAIRMAN OF THE
NATIONAL SHEEPDOG ASSOCIATION

Not right to give help to a wolf!

SHEEP

Sheeps' Rules for Wolves

No biting!

You've got to treat us nice- like.

Never, ever, to let this password
we be about to give to be used against
any sheep, anywhere.

DESTINY, ACTION, AND RESULTS

On Destiny

To each creature its own destiny;
every animal in its proper place.

REX

Farmer Hoggett knew that little ideas that
tickled and nagged and refused to
go away should never be ignored, for in
them lie the seeds of destiny.

NARRATOR

You were sent here for a reason.

PINK POODLE (TO BABE)

There's no telling
where we'll end up.

HORSE

Fate turns on a moment.

NARRATOR

Tranquillity
will prevail.

THELONIUS

On Risk

We'll run.

FARMER HOGGETT

On Expectations

Whatever it is . . .
whatever is asked of you . . .
I expect you to give of
your best.

REX

Laudatory Lines

Good pig.

FARMER HOGGETT

Beautifully done.

BABE

The pig's done it!

FERDINAND

Our Ba-a-a-a-abe!
Hoora-a-a-a-ay!

SHEEP

That'll do, Pig.
That'll do.

FARMER HOGGETT